Who's the Old Broad at the Bar?*

To Dave & April
with love
2010

Patty

Who's the Old Broad at the Bar?*

by

Katherine Baer

*Once while sitting on a barstool at the Crab Shanty Restaurant in Ellicott City, Maryland, my mother was noticed admiringly by the Italian manager Giuseppe who inquired of the bartender (my kid sister Chris), "Who's the old broad at the bar?"

ISBN 978-0-557-26607-4

These remembrances are dedicated
to my mother Edith Ruhl Finn
who found joy in many things

Contents

Born Again

Merging onto I-95 at 5:15 in the morning, I expected to share the road with some other —but not many— commuters. I was in Consultant Mode, retired but working on *my* terms, liberated by the feeling that I was in charge.

A sea of headlights flowed down the highway, enveloping me. The luxury of lifelong short commutes taunted me as I struggled to suppress the somewhat panicky feeling of being in the midst of madness. Here I was, setting out extra early, feeling a bit self-congratulatory about cutting my sleep short to assure early arrival at the presentation I was hired to make seventy miles from my condo.

But all these other drivers clutching steering wheels in the dark were regulars, and I was a mere pretender. The ding of the GPS became my obsession. It signaled an upcoming direction from Peter, my nickname for the British-accented voice I'd chosen to lead me. The soothing background of soft jazz—my usual companion—was unthinkable. I might miss a critical detail and veer off onto a ramp leading to some road to God-knows-where.

Illuminated buildings loomed on the sidelines of the highway. The recurring realization that so many people get up in what I'd always considered to be part of night jolted me. Certainly I've not lived my life oblivious to early, long-distance commuters, but the sheer quantity of them on this morning late in the summer of 2007 signaled to me that the world had changed a notch while I wasn't paying attention. The painful truth of congestion, the awareness that this morning lunacy had become necessity, fizzled in my brain.

Blinking lights are the enemy. Any sign of construction, any police presence unnerves you. The first sign of brightening taillights ahead prompts a visceral reaction. "I'm going to get stuck, creeping car length by car length." The worst thought of all, though, is the thought that you are completely at the mercy of things beyond your control.

As I hurtled along a mostly unfamiliar maze of road among lane-changing, sleep-deprived humans propelled by greed and duty, the full impact of the danger in it smacked into my brain. My back ached from hunching forward, my eyes and throat dried, and my obedience to a mechanical voice felt surreal. But I needed to be on that road—not for money as much as for the challenge.

This morning wasn't the first time I hadn't quite recognized myself.

Being widowed at the age of sixty is especially jarring. Fifty-nine-year-old widowhood would have been significantly more tolerable. Turning sixty *and* being widowed in the same year constitutes cruelty. First of all you can't possibly come to grips with the irrefutable proof that you have crossed over into "Getting Old Land," and secondly you can't possibly deal head-on with being "A Single" all of a sudden.

The amazing thing, though, is that I not only survived but have invented a new me. During most of my fifties I assumed that I would keep morphing into the comfortable, mature grandmother that I started being at fifty-one. Despite an occasional, haunting suspicion that life had another phase in store for me, my pattern seemed in place. My compass set for predictable longevity, I figured "the growing" years were behind me.

In the span of less than two years, I'd grieved, sold a house, bought a condo, retired from a thirty-year job, fallen in love again, and started a consulting business. Every day was a discovery of some sort.

"Let's Face The Music And Dance"

There may be trouble ahead
But while there's music and moonlight and love and
romance
Let's face the music and dance

Before the fiddlers have fled
Before they ask us to pay the bill and while we still have
the chance
Let's face the music and dance

Soon we'll be without the moon, humming a different
tune and then
There may be teardrops to shed
So while there's moonlight and music and love and
romance
Let's face the music and dance

Irving Berlin

Writing Desk 2008

"I like living. I have sometimes been wildly, despairingly, acutely miserable, racked with sorrow, but through it all I still know quite certainly that just to be alive is a grand thing."

Agatha Christie

About Face

True sisterhood is tested when—naked in the shower—your sister shampoos dried blood out of your hair following a facelift. Separated by ten years (she's the younger one), the two of you have shared an abundance of life adventures, but this is something else altogether.

She's fascinated. Her turn is coming. You're feeling pretty freaky. You've just had a surgeon alter your face for god's sake!

She's nervous. Her recruitment as "recovery nurse" carries both pride and squeamishness.

You're exposed, more naked than you've ever felt. And it's more than the spotlight in the shower illuminating every splotch. Your self-image is hanging out. Plastic surgery . . . the ultimate vanity? And you've just done it.

But back to the beginning.

When was the seed planted to do this thing? Was it when you turned fifty-nine, damn it. Was it the day you bought that three-way lighted make-up cosmetic mirror and stared, amazed? Was it much longer ago than that and you never recognized it?

Or maybe it was simply because you've finally learned you have to please yourself.

The toughest part is finding a surgeon you trust enough to take surgical knives to the face you've toted around for a lifetime. You devour descriptions of the procedures from *The Complete Idiot's Guide to Cosmetic Surgery* and make an appointment. Your dermatologist recommends him; your GP admires him. But it ultimately comes down to meeting him face-to-face the first time, shaking his hand, and knowing. (blink: the power of thinking without thinking.)

The countdown begins. As D-day approaches, you never completely put it out of your mind (do it, do it, do it). The scare factor rides on the edge of your brain.

Email from my daughter: "Mom, You're about to change your face, but don't ever change YOU. I love you just the way you are."

Wow. Of all the reactions, none has startled me like this one. If you can't depend on your mother being steady, steady, steady, what *can* you depend on? I'd thrown my children more curves in the last year than most mothers. Rebirth after widowhood had blossomed spontaneously from within me as an irrepressible force driven by fearless determination.

Honestly, though, once I made my decision to do it, I never turned back from it. I *wanted* to erase a few years of sadness from my face.

Determined to spare my sister and daughter hours of tedium while I was marked, prepped, and wheeled into surgery, I insisted on taking a cab to the hospital on The Big Day. The cab died an electrical-failure kind of cough-cough on the exit ramp from the expressway about a half-mile from the hospital. There wasn't a single second of "stay calm" in me. I leaped from the cab, waved down the first passing car, and jumped in. There was no cab, no circumstance in the realm of "this can't be happening" that was going to derail me from the path I was on. I was due in surgery—surgery!—and I was going to be there (superstition be damned!).

"You plastics get only top-drawer stuff," winked one assistant at 7:00 am as I expressed my expectation of nausea after anesthesia. Who wants to wake up with a new face and barf first thing? Well, I found out that barfing isn't really so bad when you've had nothing but IV fluid for a whole day. And besides . . . I woke up. Nobody got to lament at my funeral: "I knew she shouldn't have done it. I thought it was foolish, but I just didn't have the heart to tell her."

Seven hours on a surgical table. I have to keep telling myself that a whole team of people worked really hard for all those hours because I decided to do something that didn't have to be done. Bless them for being so careful.

It took me until the next day to realize that I had no pain. No pain.

I'm sure it would have been reassuring if I'd been told beforehand that I wouldn't need a single painkiller after my facelift, but I wouldn't have believed it. It wasn't until Sunday that I downed the first Advil. Now *that's* what I call talented hands.

So I bet you're wondering about that naked shower—huh?

Miraculously, Dr. K visited me at my own bedside the day after surgery and blithely explained that I should get in the shower and clean up the next day. Get in the shower under running water! Please understand that your eyes are blurry after eyelid surgery and you feel vulnerable with stitches in your eyes. Running water from a showerhead seemed as dangerous as an Amazon safari at the moment. Four showers later over the next four days, my hair returned to normal and has never pleased me more.

It's a certainty my sister will never forget applying shampoo to my stapled scalp. Perhaps this is the perfect point at which I should make something clear: second only to the surgeon in importance is the women you entrust to care for you afterward.

I didn't anticipate having so much fun while recovering. Healing doesn't negate small joys; it necessitates them.

Dr. K had sworn me to a commitment of two weeks at home after surgery, and my usual whirling dervish approach would make this a challenge. Stockpiled with books, movies, and promises from everybody to come visit, I hoped to contain myself for fourteen days post-op. My condo had been little more than a sleepover for months.

As with so many things, the key is humor. It was hysterical that I had doctor's orders not to laugh, which of course made the urge to laugh more delicious. Those I love, love to laugh. That's a big part of why I love them. The days following surgery unfolded with silliness aplenty. With the arrival of my beautiful daughter on the third day, my internal smiling doubled. One particular shared discussion of bikini waxes will be retold by the three of us with naughty glee for years.

(When left alone after four days of bountiful attention, the first thing I discovered was that a hard-boiled egg, when reheated in a microwave, will explode into a hundred pieces of shattered yolk and white when pricked with a fork. I viewed the wreckage of the exploded egg through spattered reading glasses. Only a stoic wouldn't have grinned.)

It's important to stimulate touch, taste, and smell at every opportunity: my sister placed a vase of calla lilies across from my bed and presented me with delicate solar chimes that tinkled unpredictably; I splurged on scented soaps and lotions in NYC prior to my surgery and used them with abandon; my sister cooked a special meal of celebration the second night after surgery that filled my rooms with the aroma of herbs; I wore silk and rayon to caress the skin on my body that *wasn't* sore. Burn scented candles.

No respectable woman I know can resist the impulse to give advice. So here it goes. Even though I've already said it, finding a surgeon with good hands and a good heart is the main thing. Dr. K called the night before surgery to check on me. Sure he prompted me to try for a good night's sleep, but more importantly he added, "I'm going to bed shortly myself so that I'll get plenty of rest." Bedside genius. And he called me the day after surgery, and the day after that, and the day after that. Framed notes of appreciation (adoration!) from patients line his waiting room walls. I'll take that over polished chrome and pretension any day.

Item two is also a repeat. Invite your female relatives and girlfriends to share this experience with you. They'll be curious and scared for you. They want to help. Their reactions, suggestions, and affection will contribute more to your well-being than you can imagine beforehand.

Item three: Once you've decided it's right for you, move forward with your plans and look for every opportunity to make it a positive experience. Like every event, it will have three stages: anticipation, occurrence, and recollection. Don't shortcut any one of the stages. Take pictures before, during, and after. Keep a journal.

Item four: Expect discomfort and deal with it effectively. Drink liquids—lots and lots. Soothe your eyes with gauze pads soaked in refrigerated sterile water. Mound your bed with soft pillows so that when you sink into them you have a chance of sleeping upright the first few days. Eat natural, healthy food. Use lip gloss generously.

Item five: Be grateful. Your grandmother didn't have this chance. Your mother didn't do it because "only movie stars do it." Yeah, yeah—wrinkles are proof that you've smiled a lot in your lifetime, but turning back the clock on your face feels wonderful.

For me, this turned out to be more than vanity. It has been part of moving on joyfully with the next phase of my life.

I'm loving this part of my life—the "yes" years.

Glamour mask 2009

"A woman must have money and a room of her own"

Virginia Woolf

Steerage

*Life has taught us that love does not consist
in gazing at each other, but in looking outward
together in the same direction.*

Some people are more strongly inclined to move from point A to point B in a straight path than others. I'm one of the others. I tend to meander a bit.

Don't get me wrong. I'm definitely task-oriented—one who decides to do something and generally does it—but when it comes to walking, predictability is off.

This presents a challenge for my boyfriend, who must try to maintain some semblance of conversation with me while surveying the surrounding territory, attempting to predict my sometimes erratic movements, and directing me as adeptly as possible so as to avoid potholes, puddles, people, poles, protrusions, and poop. Walking seldom reduces my urge to talk, so responding to my comments and questions ups the ante quite a bit.

Fortunate for me, our first trip to Manhattan—the ultimate test for walking couples—happened early in our relationship when Matt was so preoccupied with being "new boyfriend" charming that he must have overlooked the near-death experiences I certainly provoked. Engulfed in a frenzy of restaurant-going, theater-going Thanksgiving throngs, newfound love propelled us around the city. The euphoria induced by multiple martinis compounded Matt's job of keeping me safe. I was invulnerable . . . I was infatuated . . . I was intoxicated in the best sense of the word.

Matt's valiant, unwavering common sense signaled him that here was a woman who would require all his powers of concentration. Years of school administration were a mere prelude to the challenge of an enthusiastic girlfriend darting from one magic moment to the next. He became adept at steering me within the first year.

His techniques are varied and adaptable. Most satisfying (and pleasant) is his palm placed gently at the small of my back, with enough pressure applied to be gallant and yet reassuring. It says, "This way, Sweetheart." The 'elbow grasp' is a bit less subtle and often necessary. Like a helmsman holding a rudder, he propels me port and starboard with precision. The 'two-handed forearm grab' is reserved for near-emergencies, such as a mindless step into the path of an oncoming taxi driven by the typical NYC kamikaze.

His most accomplished maneuver, however, is the one we call 'the cowcatcher.' Much as I dislike using a bovine term in any way remotely connected to me, it's apropos. True railroaders never use the term, but to laymen, it's the wedge-shaped device attached to the front of a locomotive to deflect obstacles. Now there's a visual image you don't want to have. Anyway, Matt incorporated this advanced tactic only after a steerage experience at the end of our second Christmas season together. More about that to come.

Loading and unloading a woman into cars, buses, taxis, shuttles, and the like requires a separate set of protective skills. Good manners and an unwavering Midwest background requires that Matt oversees the series of moves (ducking the head, swiveling the torso, placing the feet, tucking in clothing) that lands my derriere satisfactorily into a passenger seat. Years of deliberate practice are needed to pull this off with aplomb. Cab drivers must be directed. Bus drivers must be paid. Gas tank fullness must be checked. The girlfriend must be settled.

I wonder if all this isn't some important metaphor for our relationship. Matt's steadfastness. My inquisitiveness. Our collective wanderlust.

Does Matt love me partly because I need a protector? Do I love Matt partly because he needs to protect?

Anyway . . . that trip during our second Christmas season together and the advent of the 'cowcatcher.' We'd selected an all inclusive resort in Punta Cana, Dominican Republic—mostly because it was warm and Caribbean, but partly because I wanted to go somewhere Matt hadn't been.

The resort was attractive. The beach was gorgeous. The food was . . . fine. Driven by a desire to "just relax" (but also by an awareness that there wasn't really much around us to see safely) we eased into sun and sand. The frenzy of Christmas back home melted into, "Where do we pick up our beach towels"?

A walk on the beach is a requirement for vacationing lovers. Since our romance started with Diane Keaton and Jack Nicholson walking on the beach in *Something's Gotta Give,* our walk was an imitation of theirs.

She: *[bending to pick up a perfect white pebble]*

         Look at this.

He: *I notice that you have bowls of those all over your house.*

She: *It's so crazy, I know.*

         But I just think they're beautiful.

He: *But why do you only pick up the white ones?*

She: *What do you mean? I don't pick up only the white ones.*

He: *So you really are crazy.*

She: *I know. I only pick up the white ones. Oh, God!*

         What does that mean?

         That I'm controlling?

         Unadventurous? What?

He: *[Smiling]*

         So you're as hard on yourself as you are on everyone else.

She: *[Looks at him askance, smiling]*

He: *[Picking up a black pebble, handing it to her]*

         Something to remember me by.

Like fictional Harry and Erica, we teased and explored the nuances of our late-in-life connection as we strolled barefoot along the edge of the surf, alternating between frivolous flirting and revealing pronouncements. Caught in the magic of lovers alone, away from everything that made us who we are, we revelled in the pleasure of placing footstep after footstep beside each others, walking toward who-knows-what, together.

There are twenty-six bones in each of our feet, nineteen of them in our toes. The protuberance from the side of the foot we call an ankle is actually the outer bump of the lower leg bone, the fibula. Its unique design makes it a very stable joint.

I wear a size six-and-a-half shoe. Matt wears a size thirteen. In stature we don't look like dance partners. Matt towers over me by more than a foot and resembles a linebacker.

If one were to speculate upon the most unlikely, unromantic occurrence that might mar the magic of our stroll, the chance of guessing what actually happened would be slim.

Some unconscious synapse caused my attention to flicker toward the dunes, attracted perhaps by some photographic possibility, some positioning of the sun. The problem was that not only did my eyes change direction, but my left foot did as well.

Although Matt had become skillful at evasive action, he didn't perceive this slight, unexpected variation in my walking pattern. His toe (the one next to The Piggy Who Didn't Go to Market) collided with my petite (but sturdy!) ankle at a right angle.

There was a crunch. There was a moment of disbelief.

The following moments demonstrated the true extent of Matt's patience and devotion. Ever the gentleman, he contained his grimaces of pain to a minimum and protested that he'd had several broken toes in the past ("No big deal.")

Broken toe! Broken toe! The realization of what I'd done presented split-second images of a third world emergency room (heaven knows how far away) and my boyfriend hobbling on crutches with a foot cast.

No, no—he insisted. Not necessary.

Why must humor be so perverse? Why, when tears and apology were certainly called for, did I have the impulse to laugh? Why, now, all these months later, am I doubled into convulsions remembering the absurdity of his giant foot banging into my tiny ankle?

For the remainder of our vacation Matt was positively stoic about his toe fracture. The appearance of an ugly black and blue swelling didn't put a dent in his pleasantness. I will be forever grateful that this test of love came when it did and not somewhere into our, say, fourth or fifth year together. (Since our longevity scale is approaching just three years and counting, I say that daringly.)

Upon our return, when I reported Matt's suffering to my son (whose admiration for Matt is huge), his eyes bulged incredulously. His almost falsetto disbelief was blurted out as, "Mom! You broke Matt's toe??!!"

Since that fateful beach walk, Matt has added the 'cowcatcher' to his repertoire. Stiff-armed . . . his hand splayed out at about a forty-five degree angle from his body, Matt fends me off whenever he senses I may be about to careen into his path.

Not even once has Matt suggested anything close to, "Why don't you watch where you're walking!"

You gotta love that.

Flamingos, Aruba 2009

*"Sometimes I wonder if men and women really suit each other.
Perhaps they should live next door and just visit now and then."*

Katharine Hepburn

Railing

Peeing away from home challenges most females. Facilities, clothing, and anatomy all conspire against us.

Since I'm of the smaller variety, I can only imagine the gyrations of women larger than me while trapped in enclosures designed by vertically inclined males.

There's an enormous balance to strike between not actually touching any bare skin to public surfaces and maneuvering your clothing to accomplish the deed. With dignity an impossibility, the best approach is speed. Get in, get out. It will be ridiculous no matter what.

For me, however, the most memorable on-the-go pee took place in spacious surroundings.

Returning by train from a romantic New York City weekend, my self-satisfaction oozed from every pore. I positioned my "I'm out to impress you" bags strategically on the seat beside me. I relished the glances at my oh, so Manhattan look – black layered on black. It was a moment of such deliciousness.

Perhaps women constantly awash with spending money often feel what I felt at that moment, but I'm pretty certain most of my pleasure emanated from its rarity. I had spent lavishly; I wore the glow of new love; I felt fabulous. For one raised to avoid excess, it was intoxicating. But even the pampered must eventually "powder their noses."

Designed to accommodate a wheelchair, the restroom at the end of my railroad car resembled a large empty closet. The mammoth sliding door felt like 400 pounds of steel. (How *would* someone in a wheelchair heave this goliath shut?)

Leaning my full body weight into the task of closing it, I felt ridiculous rather than inconspicuous, as I'd hoped. Once inside, I'm sure my snicker of self-humiliation echoed in the cavernous interior. Engrossed as I was in the effort, I failed to notice that one was expected to actually latch the door in the locked position. The monster seemed so completely and utterly shut.

I needn't explain to any female what the two-inch hover position is, and I'll have to trust that males may have some inkling. In any case, I perched upon "the throne" just as the train rounded a curve in the track. Some mischievous combination of trajectory and gravity caused the sliding door to thrust itself open along its track, revealing my half-clad body suspended as it was in mid-pee.

One lone elderly gentleman occupied a seat opposite the restroom, in full view of my exposure. He napped upon his chest as I journeyed to the restroom moments before. The velocity of the door and the resulting metallic crash upon its casing no doubt startled him into awareness. One might expect that our eyes would meet during this burlesque, but actually his eyes connected in amazement with . . .

I must digress. Prior to this trip, fascinated by yet another trend aimed at making females more Barbie-like, I dared to submit to the latest Brazilian waxing fad. I had taken it a step farther though by telling the esthetician to forego the small remnant of growth referred to as "the landing strip" and remove every follicle from my nether region. I was as bald as a ten-year-old girl.

My appearance must have given that old man a puzzling glimpse of altered womanhood. Surely at his age, he'd never seen what he now viewed just ten feet away.

I have no recollection that the door felt weighty as I slammed it shut for a second time. They tell stories of mothers who lift a car by force of a maternal adrenaline rush. But what was I to do? I couldn't stay in there all the way to the BWI station.

Hilarity replaced astonishment. Rocking with squelched laughter, I could hardly readjust my clothing.

My reappearance into the railroad car denied what had transpired. A manicured, composed female traveler emerged, her sophistication restored.

But she winked at the old gent as she passed.

Mele 2009

"To keep our faces toward change and behave like free spirits in the presence of fate is strength undefeatable."

Helen Keller

Transistor Radio

"As we move through our lives, we carry with us the stories of our childhood. We may change them, forget or deny them, smile or cry over them, but, like charms or spells, they bring back a sense of who we were and how we came to be the people we've become."

(*Legacy*, Spence)

The invention of the transistor radio was a huge breakthrough for electronics, but I couldn't have cared less for the magic of the science behind it. Like every other preteen, all I cared about was the promise of carrying music out of the house and taking it with me wherever I went.

Although the Japanese (in particular Sony) would soon dominate the portable radio market, the first transistor radio was the American made Regency TR-1, offered in October 1954 by Regency and a little known company called Texas Instruments. This first transistor radio cost $49.95 (the equivalent of about $375 in 2007 dollars).

The release of the first big rock n' roll hit, *Rock Around the Clock*, happened just months before the announcement of the first transistor radio. These parallel events opened a new world to teenagers, and I was on the brink of becoming part of the Rock and Roll Generation. By 1957 everybody knew who Elvis Presley was, and lucky kids were listening to him on their transistor radios.

I was approaching twelve at the time. That made me a sixth grader, among the oldest elementary schoolers, the kids ego-inflated but scared by the anticipation of entering Junior High the following year.

I probably started my campaign for a transistor radio before Christmas 1956, but I was still only an eleven year old then, and certainly my parents felt that was too young. However, in May 1957 I would turn twelve—an honest to goodness preteen and therefore eligible for more serious gift-giving consideration. Our plans for a summer beach rental at Cape St. Clair in Anne Arundel County made the prospect of having my very own transistor radio positively intoxicating. I fantasized about posing in the sand, my radio held to my ear in pretended disregard for my surroundings.

Whatever my parents may have discussed, the eventual plan was for my father (a studious, frugal engineer) to select my birthday present. As was the case with most couples in the 1950's, my father earned a salary and made all decisions involving money; my mother was a "homemaker," caretaker of the house and children. I'll never know if Mom had any input as to the selection of my radio other than agreeing that, yes, I could get one.

When the birthday box was handed to me, I was fairly certain what it contained. My imagining of it beforehand was of a turquoise and white plastic model, one that would look modern and sophisticated, one that would impress my friends. I tore into the wrapping paper.

The number one hit in 1957 was Pat Boone's *Love Letters in the Sand*. I was to listen to that song on my new radio over and over and over during the summer of 1957. I carved hearts into the beach with driftwood as I sang ("On a day like today, we passed the time away, writing love letters in the sand"), my radio resting on a beach towel within eyesight.

But it wasn't the radio I had dreamed about.

Nestled in the tissue paper of my birthday box was a larger-than-lunchbox size black, leatherette Emerson radio with a black carrying handle on top. It was boxy and heavy, with an enormous rectangular battery stored in a flap-door compartment in the back of the radio. If someone had taken my grandfather's big old vacuum tube floor model radio out of the parlor, replaced the tubes with transistors and compressed it in a compactor, it would have come out looking like my birthday present. It was hideous.

Looking back, I've often wondered how aware my parents were of my stunned reaction. I can only hope that I had the good grace to cover my dismay with some believability. But parents know their children with such intimacy—at least my mother did—that a twelve-year-old could hardly have pulled off a deception in the face of such crushing disappointment.

Later, alone in my room, I'm sure I cried. How could I take this ugly, awkward excuse of a radio out among my friends? The tantalizing hopes for a first boyfriend (no doubt attracted to a girl with a snazzy new transistor radio) evaporated. Our upcoming beach vacation lost its charm.

I strategized my first day on the beach as a general might plan a major battle. The only salvation was my beach towel. There was no possibility of carrying the radio tucked into my elbow as I did my books at school. No, no. This beast had to be lugged by its handle, banging at the side of my knee. But if I draped my beach towel over it, at least I could avoid full exposure. I practiced walking with it so as to give the impression that it was weightless. I learned how to swing it just a bit so that it didn't look like a box of bricks torturing my five-foot frame.

After eyeing the beach for the perfect spot—not too close to the water but certainly not too far back where the losers would sit—I positioned a second beach towel in the sand, spreading it in imitation of Sandra Dee in one of her beach blanket movies. The Emerson was carefully camouflaged under its beach towel during my maneuvers. I propped my beach bag against it to minimize its bulk, making sure the AM dial was easily reachable. I settled in, leaning against my arms behind me, one leg bent movie star style.

On previous vacations, my sister Janet would have been my companion, but now at fifteen, she'd connected with Chuck, a local with a runabout ski boat. She didn't know I existed that summer.

Luck was with me. Several boys about my age were also spending the week at Cape St. Clair with their parents, and after a couple of days one of them hovered around me. I was petite and moderately cute, enough to overcome the curse of the Emerson. Days of newly discovered flirtation enveloped me and made me giddy.

Two nights before the week would end, my mother volunteered to drive a bunch of us to and from a bonfire party in a nearby community. Our maroon 1955 Buick Special (affectionately referred to in antique car circles today as a "boat") was easily large enough.

Seated in the back, I snuggled into the outstretched arm of my first boyfriend and we "necked" (as we called it then). There was a lot of giggling and a lot of kissing. Pretty innocent stuff (no groping involved), but of course this was happening directly behind my mother, who drove stiff-backed and pretended not to hear what was obviously happening.

It's amazing how, when you are infatuated with someone, the rest of the world disappears. The boy and I were oblivious to everything else in that car. Our fellow passengers could have turned into aliens, and we wouldn't have noticed. Caressed in the bubble of first kisses, my mind abandoned every shred of manners instilled in me. I give her credit for not scolding me in front of my new friends.

When we got home, it was another story. Mom entered the bedroom where I shared a bunk bed with Janet and sat down on the edge of the lower bunk, controlled anger bursting from her. "How could you behave that way? I'm so disappointed in you, Kathy. Don't expect to go out with your friends anymore, and I don't want to see that boy around here again."

Mom hardly ever got mad. I was ashamed, humiliated, embarrassed, remorseful. I felt terrible.

And yet . . . I somehow wasn't the same girl who came to the beach—insecure about the changes happening in me, worried about being accepted, mortified by the wrong birthday present. Yeah, I was grounded for the rest of the trip, but I look back on that vacation with pleasure. I stood on a threshold the end of that sixth grade year, and when I stepped over, I wasn't really a child again.

As an adult, I've searched antique shops repeatedly for an old Emerson, hoping to replace this abomination from my past. I have no recollection of what eventually happened to my radio, but I continue my nostalgic fascination with obtaining this ghost from childhood. A recent inspiration led me to search online for that old radio. Finally my poking around led to the discovery of the model number. My dad had bought me an Emerson 842, manufactured for only five or six months in the second half of 1955—until customer reaction caused Emerson to abandon a clunky, poorly received design and replace it with a smaller plastic model 849.

I'll bet some happy salesman chuckled all the way home the day he dug that Emerson 842 out of the back of his stockroom and sold it to my father.

The Rah Bar, Jekyll Island 2009

"True enthusiasm is a fine feeling
whose flash I admire where-ever I see it"

Charlotte Bronte

A Day in the Life . . .

Two cats are indoor cats – Lizzy and Oliver. Five cats are outdoor cats – Eggie, Tod, Grayface, Fudge, and Ringo.

In order to execute an entrance into the Mud Room door, you must have a solid grasp of this information, for you will be greeted by several if not all of the outdoor cats on the exterior side of the door who will, as cats do, wriggle and slither their agile selves between your legs and feet—all the time imploring you with seductive mewling to let them in.

Simultaneously the indoor cats will greet you the second you turn the doorknob and open the door a crack big enough to cram your body through. Undoubtedly encumbered by various parcels, you dance the "don't let the outdoor cats in" dance, a maneuver worthy of a skilled contortionist. If all goes well amidst greetings and hugs and inner-house confusion, five cats (but more likely only four) will have remained out-of-doors. Almost invariably, there will be a momentary scooping up of an invading cat, the careful cracking of the door, and a hasty deposit on the porch brick. Add a bit of nasty weather to the equation and you have the makings of mayhem before your visit has officially begun.

I have a mental block about the cats' names. My daughter and the grandchildren are amazingly patient about renaming them for me almost every time I come. After this visit, however, I think the names will finally stick. Collin's delightful second grade paragraph description and accompanying drawings of the cat menagerie (done on that adorable primary paper with two solid lines divided by a dotted line for lower case letters) has been my "cheat sheet" this visit. Hey! I'm visual (and apparently cat name deficient).

I'm the guest conductor for a long weekend. The complexities of overseeing a homestead consisting of fifteen acres, a barn, horse fields populated by seven horses (yes, yes—seven cats and seven horses, but that's just the current count) rocks me.

I may be an animal lover in the ordinary sense, but I'm certainly not in the league required of farm owners—even "gentleman farms" like this one. You have to be crazed to huff up to a cold barn and muck stalls!

My twelve-year-old granddaughter Kelsey gave me a long overdue orientation to the barn. I'd been in there dozens of times, but I hadn't ever let myself *really* be in there—in the sense of figuring out how to put a halter on a horse, or fill water buckets, or double-check the stall latches.

Turns out . . . it's a good thing I finally paid attention to the details.

The boys, Patrick and Collin, left for school at the indecent time of 7:21. Fifteen minutes after middle-schooler Kelsey bounded onto her school bus and I was just settling in for checking email, I glanced up to the sight of a horse and three ponies doing laps across the front lawn.

Funny, I thought, that I'd had some inkling of this happening before my daughter and son-in-law left town. "What should I do," I'd asked, "if the horses get loose?" For some reason, this concern preoccupied me more than, "What if Collin falls out of the tree fort", or "What if Patrick breaks a bone at football practice", or "What if Kelsey runs the four-wheeler into the shed?" (You get the picture . . . Grandmothers have thousands of danger scenarios they play over and over in their heads. It's required.)

"I don't think they will," Kevin assured me, "but if they do, the best thing is to bribe them with food. They're so stupid they'll follow a handful of oats into a stall."

Good to know.

As I sprinted to the front yard (pausing for only a millisecond to consider that I really *should* replace my sandals for sneakers), I faced four wind-freaked escapees. Circling, dodging, whinnying, they eventually cornered themselves by the silo. I know I was talking, cajoling frantically. If recorded, it would sound something like, "Please, please, dear God, don't let them get up to the road!" (True confession: I'm only religious when panicked.)

I grabbed a halter from the floor of the barn, hoping I'd be able to handle it deftly despite shaky hands and a pounding heart. Miracle of miracles, the horse I attempted to halter actually let me do it and actually let me lead him (well, it turned out to be her) into the nearest fenced field.

Old, muddy-white Moony was more stubborn. She let me halter her, all right, but she wasn't about to follow me anywhere. I tugged. I tried to act tough. I pleaded. Few things make you feel as inadequate as trying to get a big animal to do your bidding and failing. I don't even want to think about the possible YouTube video a passer-by would have captured at the moment. I yanked on that halter for dear life. She planted her feet more firmly.

Aha! I remembered what Kevin had said about the bribe. Oats, oats—yes, get some! It worked like a charm. Into the stall she went.

Two more rambunctious ponies to go. That little devil, Jack. He must have been the culprit who set this in motion. I was least worried about Mickey, but even he was cantankerous. . . but . . . Oh, my God! The realization hit me that I had put Chrissy (mistaking her for the new horse Bob) into the pasture with the male horses.

I'm sure to the Stewarts, Bob and Chrissy don't look remotely alike, but to me they were both brown. In the heat of the moment, I overlooked that Chrissy has a black mane and Bob does not. Kelsey's words from the previous night came back to haunt me. "You can't put the female horses in with the male horses," she had explained, "because the males will fight over the female—even to the death." As her grandmother, I don't really want to know how much she understands the implications of that situation.

What had I done! The answer was apparent with one glance at Thor—a mammoth beast whose back I can't reach with a grooming brush. His anatomy had changed remarkably. There's just no way to put this delicately—his shlong was hanging to his knees and elongating by the moment. I had made his day. I gasped in horror, prepared to witness equestrian fornication at the least or a ghastly spectacle of males gnashing and battling to a bloody conclusion. An image of my trampled, prostrate body mixed in there somewhere.

I had to go back in the pasture and . . . and . . . rescue Chrissy? Kill myself? Prove that Grandma Linda isn't the only grandmother with guts?

At this point, Thor didn't look as if he would be willing to stand there and let me remove the object of his affection. He hovered close. I knew that if I were lucky enough to get Chrissy to follow me a second time, he was sure to follow. How would I get the gate open and then closed with an amorous goliath in pursuit? I pleaded to the heavens for a chance to see another day.

Perhaps some may scoff at my adventure as a mere trifle. But for an academic like me, this was heady stuff. For a change, I relied on muscle and moxie rather than words and wit. So for me, this was a moment to remember, and remember it I will.

All's well that ends well, they say. Chrissy ended up, unmolested, safe in her stall, and I . . . well I ended up back here, safe at my keyboard.

Grandmothering is a wonderment.

Good Feelings Farm 2008
Westminster, Maryland

*"Life begets life. Energy creates energy.
It is by spending oneself that one becomes rich."*

Sarah Bernhardt

To Wed or Not To Wed

A pair of cut-lace turquoise panties from Victoria's Secret lies crumpled into an unused wad in the back, never-used corner of my lingerie drawer. I know they're there, and I know I'll never wear them. But there they will stay.

Purchased in San Francisco prior to a performance of *Jersey Boys*, they serve as a reminder of one of the more memorable moments of an almost perfect summer trip in July of 2007.

By then, Matt and I were approaching the anniversary of our first date on July 23, 2006. The newness of the first year was untarnished. Every delicious month had convinced us that this was the real deal. We'd progressed through the first infatuation stage to the couple stage and stood upon the precipice of commitment.

After four seasons, the question of "Where is this going?" bubbled to the surface. I'd felt it coming. Multiple moments—some as subtle as a friend's inquisitive cocked eyebrow, some as blatant as gazing into a diamond-laden jewelry window together—wove an invisible speculative undercurrent into our relationship. I suppose he was less aware of it than me, but certainly he felt it, too.

According to Steve Harvey in his bestseller *Act Like a Lady, Think Like a Man*, a woman should know if a man is serious about her by the way he introduces her. If he introduces her something like, "I'd like you to meet _____", then he's not committed to her (or at least not sure). But if he introduces her to a group of people (friends, family, neighbors, etc.) something like, "This is my girlfriend _____" then he's staking his claim and letting any and all other males know to keep off. I'd had that assurance plenty of times, and we'd had "future talk" . . .

plans of things we wanted to do together. But together is a loaded word.

And so we ended up on a trip that started in Las Vegas where I had presented a workshop and was booked into a plush bathrobes kind of luxuriousness. kind of luxuriousness. We sprawled, we indulged, we wallowed. It's important to mention that up to this time Matt and I stayed first in separate rooms and then in separate beds whenever we traveled. There are some bottom line arrangements of paramount importance to me, the most paramount of which is that a man and a woman over thirty shouldn't have to share a bed or a bathroom. At home—his or mine—this was the arrangement.

You get to the point where you want your space. Young lovers aren't happy unless super-glued together, but older lovers understand the beauty of privacy and boundaries. While traveling, some compromises had to be made, but in this spacious room we occupied at the Venetian, we didn't feel compromised at all.

It's also important to mention that at this stage in our romance, we carefully avoided any acknowledgement of bodily functions. This requires an intricate set of maneuvers that enables you to use the same hotel bathroom (but never, never at the same time!) without violating a certain mystique.

Come to think of it, why hasn't somebody written a detailed etiquette-style pamphlet about disguising bodily functions with aplomb? I'll bet every woman over thirty would buy copies for herself and every girlfriend worth a birthday card. My personal favorite—a throwback to the fifties—is the running faucet. Why is it that most young folks don't think the sound of "doing # 1" is something to be cloaked anymore? My bet goes to the Madison Avenue maniac who couldn't let "that time of the month" stay a mystery.

I digress. But eventually you'll understand why, when we returned from this trip, that a certain boundary had been breached and that we scrupulously avoid mention of it since.

The digestive system is an almost comical but wondrous concoction of tongue, esophagus, stomach, and intestines. In the movie *Tom Jones*, the suggestive nuances of chewing caused the uppermost part of the digestive tract to become positively sensational.

Under normal circumstances, a person isn't aware of the movements of food down the 20-some-foot digestive tract, but we all have various shuttering memories of occasions when we *were* aware of the serpentine journey. If you've been enormously lucky, you've never had a date become aware of some torturous gastric malady—one that would necessitate ungodly sounds, hasty exits, or pathetic apologies. Let's face it . . . it's just plain ghastly that the delightful intake of certain delicacies ends with such an indelicate exit. How is one to maintain dignity when one's body is just so much plumbing?

A tour of the Napa Valley followed Las Vegas. Sun, wineries, a sassy BMW rental car, picnics in bed. Fabulous. A trip worthy of the description perfect.

San Francisco followed the Napa Valley. I underestimated the smallness of a room in Union Square, but as is typical of an historic city, our room was two feet bigger than a closet. The bathroom was the most daunting obstacle; it was nearly impossible to negotiate a door closing. Both of us squirmed as we surveyed the prospects of a night plastered together in a bed too small and a bathroom nothing short of ridiculous. This would be a test.

Relieved to get out of the room as quickly as possible, we delighted in the unexpected tickets we'd bought for *Jersey Boys*—a show so popular when we'd last been in NYC that we'd failed to score. The night seemed more and more promising with second cocktails. Several trendy and expensive shops bordered the theater, so we occupied ourselves poking around for sexy little luxuries. Aha! A Victoria's Secret. As we teased and nuzzled our way through the abundance of panties, perfumes, and peek-a-boo playthings, an overly attentive saleswoman attached herself to us, obviously convinced we were an easy sale.

Her suspicion was that we were either honeymooners or about-to-be-marrieds. Out popped the question. No, we demured, we're not here to get married. Again she asked, convinced—I guess—that we were being coy. The second time was the catalyst for choosing something (anything) and making our escape. Thus the turquoise panties, boy-cut as they were and completely wrong for my body. Intoxication makes you forget practicalities such as the fact that only under-weight, long-legged women can wear low-slung, hip-hugging panties well. They seemed just perfect at the moment, even more so because they were expensive. Excessively giddy from alcohol and possibilities, I feigned indifference to the price.

Time for dinner before the show.

Matt defers to me about restaurant choice more often than not, and in this case the choice was all mine. A nearby informal eatery—worn wood, Old World charm, German-Irish aromas—lured me inside, Matt following noncommittally. A lengthy buffet along one side of the room offered steam tray upon steam tray of various hearty comfort food—sausages, cabbage, potatoes, pork, sauerkraut, spaetzle, wurst-this and wurst-that.

(Did I mention cabbage?) Raffinose is a complex sugar abundant in certain carbohydrates. (Did I mention cabbage?) Unlike protein, carbohydrates are responsible for most of the gas produced in the digestive tract while food is being broken down for absorption. (Did I mention cabbage?)

Matt's a man who appreciates food zestfully. I watched with pleasure as he stacked his plate. What more could we add to this delightful last night of our trip? (Well, yeah . . .) We sat at a less than glamorous table (the whole restaurant was less than glamorous), but it didn't matter. Conversation would be the main event. I wish that I could accurately recall how the conversation actually unfolded, but alcohol makes talk hazy in recollection.

Recounting the details of the Victoria's Secret foray, I think we danced around and around the word marriage. One jewelry store we'd passed earlier featured several amusing windows suggesting, for example, what size engagement ring a woman considers the right size alongside the engagement ring a man thinks is adequate. All this was fuel for the fire.

How do we pick the moment for romantic decision-making? The complex bombardment of rational considerations (taxes, social security, property ownership, wills, in-sickness-and-in-health, etc.) collide with pure emotions. Did I actually ask Matt, "Do you think we should get married?" In any case,

Matt didn't seem on the brink of a proposal, and I discovered that with the idea on the table, so to speak, I really wasn't eager to be on the receiving end of a proposal. We were content—no, no, much more than content—with what we had going on. There! It was out in the open and it was a relief.

Matt adorns almost everything he eats. Most of the time this involves ketchup, but it can be mayonnaise, gravy, barbecue sauce, or (in this case) mustard. As we talked the marriage talk, Matt hoisted a large bottle of Bavarian mustard over his plate and squirted abundantly, smothering his sausage-cabbage combination with a yellow-brown coating. Eating rapidly is the norm for him, but the anxiety generated from tickling around the edges of a girlfriend possibly asking for a proposal quickened his pace. Forkful after forkful was scooped, accompanied by gulps of air as he negotiated the perils of this tricky conversation.

During the performance of *Jersey Boys*, Matt was quiet. The turmoil roiling inside him was unknown to me. His gastric juices must have been on hyper-drive—churning, churning, churning. At intermission, my mind wandered ahead to the intimacy of that bed back in Union Square. Matt's mind probably focused on that miniscule bathroom with the wedged in toilet.

I became aware of Matt's distress after midnight, when his groans awoke me and I discovered that he had spent the time I slumbered trying to escape the throes of acute intestinal blockage. His mention of the Emergency Room jolted me to attention. The last night of our magical trip was to be spent in the horrible place of all horrible places.

St. Francis's Hospital was a short cab ride away, during which I took measure of the extent of my hangover. The surrealism of it all was magnified by my one-too-many nausea. The entrance of the turn-of-the-century building (no, not this century, the last one) didn't bode well. Perhaps our arrival in the wee hours made it seem sootier, mustier than it really was.

Crime dramas seem to exaggerate the seamy underbelly of humanity, but a real-life visit to an inner-city emergency room convinces you that no, we're not all middle America. The mangy collection of dysfunctional, damaged characters we waded into was tempered only by the heroic medical souls who face the challenge of taming the chaos daily. Physical suffering is compounded by undeniable evidence of mental instability. One poor soul chanted, "I'm not crazy!" throughout our stay. To this day, when some ludicrous situation arises, Matt and I look at each other and mimic her.

Our attending nurse repeatedly called me Mrs. Considering the context of the preceding evening, it seemed inevitable. She was Irish and obviously eager to make like-minded folks as comfortable as possible under the circumstances. Matt maintained an amazing degree of poise in a too small, tie-string hospital gown on an inch-thick, dilapidated gurney.

Gastric suction was offered as a remedy. Imagine trying to be pleasant (forget romantic!) while having a plastic tube pushed into your nose and down your throat so that the contents of your stomach can be sucked out by a machine making disagreeable sounds in front of your girlfriend. Left alone once the tube was in place, it's amazing how almost normally we had a conversation during the interlude required for all the sucking to take place.

No candlelight, no music, no roses. Just two people in love who had discovered that yes, we'd made a commitment.

Perhaps the ER was a necessary absurdity for us. That first year of romance was splendid, but we both knew that love must become something tougher in order to last. Anybody can be happy when all goes right. It's the screw-ups, the missteps, the unexpected downturns that determine how much you want to be together.

Seniors are the fastest growing demographic among unmarried couples, and we're among them. We don't beat ourselves up about cohabitating without wedlock. To wed or not to wed? We've answered that question for now. If someday we feel we need to answer it again, we will.

The Waldorf-Astoria Hotel, NYC 2008

"Ideally, couples need three lives; one for him, one for her, and one for them together."

Jacqueline Bisset

BJC

Two lovely little stories involving fruit and bosoms came into my life in the past year or so. The first came from Matt's childhood when he and his brother worked at a fruit stand in Indiana. They witnessed a buxom matron selecting plums—two for the bag, one for her brassiere; two for the bag, one for her brasserie. After their callow sensibilities recovered from the shock of this semi-sexual thievery, they reported the occurrence to their employer, who offered a sure-fire remedy. The next time the matron bought plums, they were to place one of their thumbs surreptitiously on the scale's edge in proportion to what they guessed she had pilfered.

The second story involves a good-natured new friend whose Italian roundness, including an ample bosom, bears witness to her culinary skills. Her grandfather, once a fancy fruit purveyor in Baltimore's Lexington Market, taught her to appreciate and savor the delights of kiwifruit, pineapples, mangoes, and the like. Her kitchen never lacks a variety of juicy produce.

While preparing recently for a trip to Las Vegas and pressed for time prior to a flight, she found that a banana, a pineapple, and a kiwifruit remained uneaten on her counter. A single woman, she had no recourse other than to eat as much of it as she could. Tradition forbid disposal of perfectly good fruit. Down went the banana and the pineapple, but then, too full to continue, she dropped the kiwifruit into her brassiere for later.

Eight hours pre-flight, airtime, and shuttle arrangements later, she lugged her suitcase to the reception desk of the glossy resort and presented herself to the desk clerk. While filling out the proper forms, she leaned against the marble counter and re-discovered the kiwifruit, long enveloped safely in its warm cocoon. The startled clerk watched with his "I've-seen-everything eyes" as she reached in and retrieved the delicacy. Certainly he managed a spot-on mimic of her giggled exclamation as he retold the event at Happy Hour later. Breasts and Vegas are usually more glamorous matches.

Both these stories amuse me. They connect with a change that's come over me of late . . . one long overdue, I'd say. Julia Child may have been thirty-two when she discovered cooking, but you can double that number for me.

I was a high school senior in 1963 when Albert Finney's now-famous cinematic food orgy debuted and made Tom Jones the best-known historical bachelor in America. As he sat across from Mrs. Waters in the Upton Inn, wordlessly and lustfully consuming an enormous meal, audiences squirmed with pleasure and then went home to romp in bed accompanied by the contents of their refrigerators.

Unaware at the time that I was crippled gastronomically, I entered my adulthood with an aversion to one of the most feminine of wiles—the ability to use food as seduction.

My sister Janet and I, the oldest and second oldest of five children, inherited birth-order chores. It was our daily duty to prepare a family meal and clean it up afterward. Sure, Mom cooked Sundays, for company, and special occasions, but the routine of dinner preparation was delegated to us. We didn't purchase the food, which probably disconnected us from the vital "gathering" component of cooking. The menu and the ingredients were predetermined; we were the grunts.

Never did I feel joy while toiling in the kitchen. It was perfunctory. Typical of suburban American families, we ate formulaically: a meat entrée, a vegetable, a starch, and rolls. The only spices in the kitchen were those McCormick provided in jars, save for the spearmint we grew in the yard to add to the nightly iced tea. Butter went on the potatoes and bread. Salt and pepper went on most everything else. And yes, we often had Jello for dessert. Squirting Ready Whip out of the aerosol can was as exciting as it got.

The arrival of Julia Child's *Mastering the Art of French Cooking* in 1961 might have been noticed by my mother's Homemaker's Club, but it failed to change the practices of our 1960s kitchen in Catonsville, Maryland. This can partially be attributed to the unexpected fourth and fifth births in my family. Once my mother produced a boy, my brother Carl, four years after I was born, that was supposed to be the end of the line. But hey, this was before the pill. Anyway, when Julia Child came along and showed housewives a manner of cooking more appetizing than they ever imagined, band-aids and boo-boo's dominated our home, not boeuf bourguignon.

I married young, as did Janet. We reproduced efficiently and mirrored the household ways of our mother. Devoted and energetic just as she was, we became young suburban wives and mothers. Gourmet food wasn't on our radar screens. Wholesome food was. I served meatloaf with mashed potatoes regularly; I served hamburgers with mac 'n cheese even more regularly. I served spaghetti sauce out of a jar over "spaghetti noodles" (as I called them then). The fine points of cooking pasta seemed confined to my friends of Italian origin, whose Mediterranean magic enabled them to sample their original tomato sauce concoctions from a wooden spoon, add spices at will, and toss a strand of pasta against the wall to test its doneness.

One thing my mother did really well was pies, cakes, and Christmas cookies. Like most women of her generation, she always baked our favorite cakes for our birthdays, produced at least one fresh pie per week, and devoted herself to scrumptious tins of various cookies baked for weeks prior to December. To this day I remember the thrill of sneaking downstairs to pry open lids and sneak out a cookie, one of each kind, from the supposedly off-limits stash. Even so, to the bakery I went rather than pass on the tradition.

Cooking continued to be a chore, something undertaken as an endless cycle of uninspired treks to the grocery store, two handfuls of tried-and-true menus recycled over and over again.

Whenever a friend arrived for a party with a "homemade" dish, I secretly considered her motivation somewhat questionable. Didn't she have something more interesting to do with her time? Even though everyone always exhibited pleasure and offered praise for these "homemade" dishes, I dismissed all but the most functional cooking as something not worth the time and effort. I've said a hundred times in my life, "You spend hours in the kitchen cooking, and it's gulped down in minutes. There's no reward in cooking. I don't like it."

Confession time. I've owned a garlic press for less than a week. Ever.

Uh-oh. Now the truth will come gushing out. I once threw out a bottle of extra virgin olive oil because it got too old sitting in my pantry. I've never owned more than eight spices (in jars, of course) at one time in my life.

It's something about doing things with abandon. Apparently cooking is one of the things in life, like sex, you must do with abandon or it's just not that good. I've been in a culinary straitjacket since I was about eleven. Did I always secretly feel that I'm too disciplined to give myself over to something so messy?

Women's liberation, a term first used a year after I graduated, means a lot of different things to a lot of people, including me. One of the things I've screwed up in my life is confusing cooking with boredom and obligation. But it's never too late to change your mind.

Change sometimes sneaks up on you, but more often than not, it's more of a melding of several things. (I wonder why cooks are never told to *meld* the butter with the eggs and sugar?) Anyway, my change of attitude has resulted from the combination of A) my abundant energy teaming up with my newfound abundant leisure B) my reading of the book *Julie and Julia*, followed by the movie of the same name C) the gradual influence of several people in my life who must enjoy cooking for *some* reason, and most importantly, D) my general zest for life because I'm so damn happy in love. (I just discovered, by the way, that zest is a cooking term! Who knew?)

In other words, the time was ripe. (And tomatoes and peaches and zucchini were ripe. If the intoxication of cooking doesn't grab you in late summer, there's no hope.)

Funny thing about cookbooks. They always had the appeal of, say, Vaseline for me. Since I saw *Julie and Julia*, I've spent hours (hours!) clipping and deciphering recipes from *Food & Wine* magazine. Matt's son Tom, an enthusiastic cook, sent me a subscription to it. Probably good he didn't know that within my family circle, everyone knew if you gave me a cookbook for a present, it would be received like Sarah Jessica Parker getting Keds.

I had one hard-and-fast rule about recipes. If there were more than six ingredients . . . forgetaboutit. When a couple of my friends see my new container herb gardens out on the deck, they're going to say, "Who *are* you?"

Don't get me wrong. If you asked my kids if they were at all deprived during their childhoods, they wouldn't mention my cooking. I was adequate. I provided. What I've now come to regret is that I couldn't find any joy (abandon?) about food that I could have passed along to them. Perhaps they'll find it for themselves.

Isn't it amazing that one of the great joys of life gets people so damned tangled up? People starve themselves and people stuff themselves. I've usually been able to hover just right of the middle of those two extremes, but it occurs to me at last that my relationship with food has been stilted.

Unless this newfound preoccupation grows like a fever within me—which I doubt given my unremitting propensity for moderation—you won't find me boning a duck anytime soon. However, I did have an experience at lunch the other day that made me realize there's no turning back. At a favorite tasty restaurant, I ordered one of their specialties, a barbecued chicken salad on whole grain bread. It was impossible to stop thinking it was mildly disappointing. I went home and fixed some that left theirs in the dust.

I think I'll mosey out on the deck and snip some lemon thyme or pineapple sage.

So what's for dinner?

French Quarter shop, New Orleans 2009

"It is sad to grow old but nice to ripen."

Brigitte Bardot

Star Struck

"You know how to whistle, don't you Steve?
You just put your lips together and blow."

Lauren Bacall, as Slim, to Humphrey Bogart in
To Have and Have Not (1944)

I married at a ridiculous age. Sure, there were lots of people who knew something about life during the '60s, but not sheltered nineteen-year-olds from the suburbs like me. You'd think Kennedy's assassination might have given me a clue that the world wasn't all peaches 'n cream, but I was on a path I never doubted.

Anyway, my new in-laws fascinated me. With only two children compared to five in my family, my mother-in-law got to shop at Hutzler's and buy a new dress once a month. She played cards and went out to lunch. My mother operated in a never-ending cycle of diapers. I thought it downright amazing when my husband's mother asked what grade I'd gotten on a Biology test I'd told her about the weekend before. My mother didn't even register that I was taking Biology.

But there are limits to admiration. I think one huge disenchantment occurred the first Christmas. I sat in my in-laws living room, neat piles of well-wrapped presents surrounding us. My mother-in-law distributed the packages one-by-one, and all of us sat with our stacks at our feet—obediently deferential, awaiting her signal to begin the unwrapping ceremony.

Once it began, the whole process took about fifteen breathless minutes. The hours of walking the mall; stressing over what would be tasteful *and* appropriate; watching over the diminishing dollars allotted for the extravaganza; wrapping the acquisitions in rolls of reindeer, or Santas, or snowflakes;

stashing and inventorying the loot; anticipating reactions to thoughtful selections—all boiled down to moments of ripping and tearing and thanking.

The presence of a large green trash bag was the centerpiece for the event. My mother-in-law was scrupulous about scooping up ribbon and paper before they settled on the floor, stuffing them determinedly in the trash bag, almost as denial that they ever existed.

We sat with fixed smiles over our sweaters and colognes. I longed for the chaos of my family Christmas event.

My family doesn't *have* Christmas. We *do* Christmas.

I'm not sure how it all started, but we seem to have mastered the art of having fun on Christmas. I say that with some trepidation for fear that one year won't measure up, but so far, we've had more than forty years of consecutive exuberant celebrations.

My children have had children, and it won't be too long before they have children . . . and still it holds. It's as if this day at the end of each year symbolizes an unshakeable optimism among us. We're not without sorrows, but each of us is aware of the blessing of unity and connection.

Fun is at the core of it all. Christmas without it is unthinkable. We recount our favorite moments as if they are somehow sacred.

"Remember the time . . ."

The adults enjoy themselves more that the kids at our Christmas party, and in fact, the kids seem to anticipate their rite-of-passage into the "adult exchange," the swapping of gifts between two ever-changing partners guided by an ever-changing theme each year. The theme is selected with great consideration on the beach at the end of each summer. One year it was an alphabet Christmas (select a gift or gifts that begin with the same letter as the first letter of your partner's name). I think I got a kite and kitchen mitts that year. One year it was a crazy hat Christmas; one year a Chesapeake Christmas; one year homemade Christmas . . .

We all understand that the actual gift is only part of the ritual. The *presentation* of the gift is as important. Songs, poems, skits, displays, etc. are essential to the merriment. Our mother (now departed), attired in a mini skirt and Rolling Stones "tongue" t-shirt, once constructed a giant papier mache stone which she rolled into the room while presenting her gift to a Mick Jagger fan in our group.

Last year was a birthday Christmas, meaning that you got something from your partner representing the year you were born. Although painful to admit, I was born in 1945 (I always pretend to be a Baby Boomer, but my conception occurred many months before the wave of copulation following the return of troops at war's end.) My sister Chris got my name for the exchange.

As a ringleader of our yearly festivities, I present an intimidation factor in the exchange (or so I'm told). Chris was immediately aghast at the prospect of having to create a gift for me and was vocal about her feelings.

"Oh, God!" she moaned. "I've got Kathy."

Admittedly, from my viewpoint, there's a certain amount of surprise and smugness about such revelations. However, 2008 had been a tough year for Chris, and I felt uneasy that she felt pressured.

As the holidays got closer and closer, I got hints she was suffering over the lack of an idea for my present. In my family, you just don't cop out. You've gotta come through.

Turns out . . . she pulled off the best Christmas present I ever got.

When the birthday theme for Christmas 2009 was announced, some family members thought you had to connect to the actual date rather than just the year of birth. That would have been tough. When I was born on May 16, 1945, Allied troops were engaged in the largest amphibious assault in the Pacific on the island of Okinawa. After the Japanese bombing of Pearl Harbor, Allied forces were pressing toward mainland Japan for what everyone anticipated would be a horrible struggle. The eighty-two day battle for Okinawa raged while I howled my first hello at Women's Hospital in Baltimore.

Six days later, on May 21, 1945, news broke about the wedding of a glamorous Hollywood couple, and everyone (surely even my mother, with a new infant and a four-year-old toddler) took notice. Glamour was an especially precious commodity during the war years. It softened some of the daily tragedies.

And so, when forty-five year old Humphrey Bogart (of legendary *Casablanca* and *Maltese Falcon* fame) married a twenty-year old Lauren Bacall, the starlet who stole his heart, war-weary people were either thrilled or scandalized—both of which served as welcome distraction.

Bogie and Bacall sizzled. Their love affair symbolized everything forbidden and undeniable. Bogie divorced his third wife to marry the gorgeous, leggy ingénue he referred to as "the love of his life." Bacall was known for "the look," a sultry expression oozing sexuality. (In fact, "the look" was born when Bacall, excessively nervous for her first screen test, sought to control her shaking by pressing her chin against her chest and tilting her eyes upward.)

In February 1945, at the urging of a publicist, Bacall perched atop a piano played by then Vice-President Harry Truman. Within months, President Roosevelt was dead from a heart attack and Truman was sworn in as the 33rd President. At his first briefing, Truman was informed of a top-secret project, The Manhattan Project, that turned theory into reality in the form of the first atomic bomb. Two months after the day of my birth, the most destructive weapon ever devised by mankind exploded in the desert of New Mexico on July 16, 1945. Truman was charged with deciding whether or not to use the "unthinkable" weapon in an effort to end the terrible war.

He decided "yes".

It's amazing how ancient that amazing year 1945 now seems. (I was tutoring a high school student last year when one of my favorite Hollywood legends died. When the boy arrived, I commented that I was sad because I'd just heard Paul Newman died. "Who's that?" he asked. This kind of thing happens to me all the time these days.)

My children, and now my grandchildren, know about Humphrey Bogart and Lauren Bacall not because they actually experienced them, but because at our Christmas party 2009, they arrived as figments of the imagination in a green Dodge truck—decorated as if for their wedding day.

My sister Chris made it happen. From a mere suggestion on my part, she researched the Bogie-Bacall story (hey, she's ten years younger) and decided my present should be presented with flair. Aided and abetted by her boyfriend Eric, who came up with the astonishing stroke of good luck that his farm truck down at their place in Virginia was a 1945, she planned and executed the most amazing "Try-to-Top-THIS" in the history of our family shenanigans.

Towed from Onancock, Virginia to Westminster, Maryland "my" Bogie and Bacall truck was decked out with tinsel and pictures so that everyone was transported back to another era when one very hot couple made America sit up and take notice. I've never been more astounded. The night was frigid and magical. Kids piled in the truck bed, and I was taken on a circuit ride, feeling as childishly delighted as I've ever felt.

"You got a TRUCK ?!!" blurted one astonished family member when she arrived on the scene a few moments after the rest of us. Yes, I got a truck. Not to keep in actuality, mind you, but forever in my heart.

What I *did* get to keep is a boxed set of the four movies Bogie and Bacall made together: *To Have and Have Not* (1944), *The Big Sleep* (1946), *Dark Passage* (1947), and *Key Largo* (1948). I've watched each of them once so far but will do so time and time again. Mostly though, I got the biggest pile of love from my younger sister. I smile every time I think about it.

Matt and I have been sharing a marvelous love story of our own for just over three years now, and our families recognize the blessing of it, not only to the two of us but to everyone who surrounds and supports it. Happiness begets happiness. Our romance exists in a smaller universe than Bogie and Bacall's, but it is real, and powerful, and important.

We fell in love over a movie on our first date. We wallow in Hollywood stories, savoring new movies and old, waiting for the next Oscars and Emmys and Tonys. We're never happier than leaning into each other shoulder-to-shoulder, whispering shared observations at a Broadway play, over popcorn at a movie, or under the covers before bedtime.

Celebrating Bogie and Bacall's passion for one another was the perfect gift for me. It encapsulated the excitement I feel daily for being loved so well, this far down the road.

" . . .*people universally tend to think that happiness is a stroke of luck., something that will maybe descend upon you like fine weather if you're fortunate enough. But that's not how happiness works. Happiness is the consequence of personal effort. You fight for it, strive for it, insist upon it, and sometimes even travel around the world looking for it. You have to participate relentlessly in the manifestations of your own blessings. And once you have achieved a state of happiness, you must never become lax about maintaining it, you must make a mighty effort to keep swimming upward into that happiness forever, to stay afloat on top of it. If you don't, you will leak away your innate contentment.*"

Thanks, Chris.

1945 Truck

"We are all here for a spell; get all the good laughs you can."

Will Rogers

A Romance of Roses

*And why it's good to believe in Santa Claus

I've lost count.

Perhaps if I'd known in the beginning, I would have kept a dated record of them—an action very much in character for me, but who knew?

Perhaps the actual record of them belongs where it is. Heart implants aren't always surgical. Gestures lodge into the tissue more completely.

In this case, accuracy isn't that important anyway. Forty-two months stretch between July 2006 and December 2009. The first arrived after the first date: a dashing, heart-stopping display that might have unnerved a more timid woman. I surveyed them repeatedly, astonished they surpassed the stereotypical dozen count. This was more than "I'm interested." This was a lusty display of romance, presented publicly for all to see. In earlier times, a lady would have dispensed a doorman to rebuff the delivery as protection for her reputation.

For the first year, one arrived every month, whimsically and unpredictably. Since I worked in a three-story office, the arrivals were witnessed and remarked upon by every worker between the receptionist's desk and my third floor cubicle on the opposite side of the building. Because only the most senior professionals warranted closed-door offices, I resided in an open space devoid of privacy. Each spectacular bouquet perched in public view after its arrival. (Well, yes . . . I didn't *have* to place them on the top of my file cabinets, but they were so much less crowded than on my desk.) They became semi-scandalous after several months of nonstop appearances, prompting one rather proper co-worker to blurt, "What are you doing to that man !!?"

I chuckle to think of the boyfriends and husbands who suffered for my roses. Even if they responded guiltily to veiled suggestions that they weren't being romantic enough, their attempts at flower giving paled in comparison to the size and frequency of the bouquets that decorated my life.

And there was always a grand symbolism added to the abundance of the eighteen beauties. Always regal and exotic, a single rose of differing color dominated the center of each bouquet—a representation of one superior to all others. Always noticed, this single deliberate message increased the curiosity of witnesses to my good fortune.

Before Matt (one way I section my life's chronology), I was somewhat immune to the romantic mystic of the rose. My practical heritage led to the misbegotten notion that roses were expensive and ephemeral and therefore a frivolous luxury. "Give me something that lasts," I'd tend to say.

But there was the House of York and the House of Lancaster, and I was entranced by the political intrigue of roses.

> *Let him that is a true-born gentleman,*
> *And stands upon the honor of his birth,*
> *If he suppose that I have pleaded truth,*
> *From off this briar pluck a white rose with me.*

(Shakespeare -The Duke of York in
Henry VI, Part I)

I read about the mythology surrounding Aphrodite's birth when she first emerged from the sea and the earth produced roses to show that it could compete with her perfect beauty.

I read about the symbolism of rose thorns in *Paradise Lost* and gazed upon Notre Dame's Rose Window in Paris. I marveled at the stories of Napoleon's Josephine and her magnificent rose gardens containing all the known varieties of roses in her time. (I heard she often carried a rose to lift to her lips when she smiled, concealing her imperfect teeth.)

Literature was a proper venue for roses—but my living room? Give me some humble daisies for special occasions. The Romans could scatter rose petals with abandon at their celebrations, but don't even think about scattering rose petals in my boudoir just for the hell of it.

And then there was always Robert Burns' "luve" like a red, red rose. That poem never turned me on (pardon the phrase). Expensive perfume made from rose oil? I don't think so.

But then Matt started sending roses, over and over again until my head spun with the shear madness of the excess. Is too much of a good thing wonderful?

Damn right.

Every woman alive should feel the way I've come to feel about Matt's roses. They are an unabashed declaration of his love for me. They reward me, they honor me, they flatter me. At the end of the first year, just when I thought I couldn't be more thunderstruck by the surprise and abundance of them, Matt sent a gigantic bouquet of twenty-seven red and pink roses on our first "anniversary." Count them, he said. One-two-three-four-five-six-seven pink ones. Twenty red ones. Get it? The anniversary of our first date is July 27. As the song says, some people wait a lifetime for a moment like this.

"Love may make the world go 'round, but it's romantic love that makes the ride worthwhile. We need love, but we crave romance (just like you need broccoli, but you crave chocolate!) It's romantic love that allows you to say emphatically "I'm in love with you," instead of merely, "I love you."

(Gregory Godek, *1001 Ways To Be Romantic*)

Matt is outrageously romantic. But he is also practical, disciplined, and trustworthy. What a combination. And let's not forget that the word ROSE is an anagram for EROS. Matt's roses make for blushes. He understands more than anyone else I know that life is too short not to live it with abandon. We can't hold on to the infatuation of the first year (nobody can), but we live our love affair with careful attention to flair and fun.

There is a moment in the play *Peter Pan* when the audience is asked to revive the dying fairy Tinkerbell. "If you believe in fairies, clap your hands." Invariably, the audience breaks into applause. I think if there were a play during which the audience was entreated "If you believe in romance, clap your hands" the same reaction would occur. We know the world is a tough place, and we know love and justice won't always prevail, but believing in the unbelievable is healthy and good. I still believe in Santa Claus, and because of Matt I still believe in romance.

When I look in your yes
I see the wisdom of the world in your eyes
I see the sadness of a thousand goodbyes
When I look in your eyes

And it is no surprise
To see the softness of the moon in your eyes
The gentle sparkle of the stars in your eyes
When I look in your eyes

In your eyes
I see the deepness of the sea
I see the deepness of the love
The love I feel you feel for me

Autumn comes, summer dies
I see the passing of the years in your eyes
And when we part there will be no tears, no goodbyes
I'll just look into your eyes

Those eyes, so wise
So warm, so real
How I love the world
Your eyes reveal

Naples, Florida 2008

"Don't cry because it's over . . . Smile because it happened."

Dr. Seuss

There is a girl inside

There is a girl inside.
She is randy as a wolf.
She will not walk away and leave these bones
to an old woman.

She is a green tree in a forest of kindling.
She is a green girl in a used poet.

She has waited patient as a nun
for the second coming,
when she can break through gray hairs
into blossom

and her lovers will harvest
honey and thyme
and the woods will be wild
with the damn wonder of it.

Lucille Clifton